My Role As A Church Trustee Study Series

The Keepers And Protectors Of God House

Dr. Joseph R. Rogers, Sr.

i. Dedication

Again the Lord has grace me the opportunity to share with the body of Christ. This time He has encouraged my heart to share some vital information concerning the **Church's Trustee Ministry.**

This is an important part of the local assembly, even though this position is not biblically; yet its need in the local assembly is vital to the existence and operation of the local church.

It is when **"Trustees"** truly understand their roles in the local assembly that property and other assets of the church is safe; as it relates to legal actions and people's protection.

So, it is with humility and reverence that I dedicate this book to all **"Trustees"** of the local church. Even though your ministry may sometime seem to be less important; I want to encourage you to keep the Lord's House with reverence, commitment and loyalty.

Even those this is not a divine call position; its important is without question. Serve well and the Lord will reward you as he has stated in his word.

God Bless,

Dr. Joseph R. Rogers, Sr.

Table Of Contents

ii. Introduction

Though the **"Trustees Ministry"** is necessary for the effective and efficient operation of a local church body, it is not a biblical office. Trustees are a State mandate whose responsibility is to the physical property of the church.

The Role of a Church Trustee is described as being a faithful steward over God's household affairs. They manage with openness to new ideas and creativity while leading the congregation in a direction of sound decision making.

Trustees are property managers, financial advisors, and legal officers for the trust they direct. Their main responsibility is to model and teach principles of good workmanship.

Trustees convey and maintain the physical assets of the local church ministry and motivate the congregation to revere and make use of their facility for the church's worship experience and other ministries for the community.

The trustee demonstrates sound management skills and judgment as it relates to the church's property.

Trustees function as the fabric of the church and as a communication link between pastor, executive board, board of directors and members of the congregation.

The trustee system dates back to the 400's in the Catholic Church in the United Kingdom. Its purpose and duties are somewhat different today. At its conception the Eleventh Council of Carthage requested that the civil power appoint five officers for their current ecclesiastical properties.

Previously the church administrators were divided into three or four portions. The newly appointed executors were to share their responsibilities as administrators with the understanding that every action was under approval from the local church body.

The employment of trustees or laymen with clerics became the norm all over the country. In England they were called church-wardens and were chosen by the parish priest and parishioners.

They administered the temporalities of the parish under the direct supervision of the churches' bishop. As trustee-ism spread throughout the nation the church began to have problems with laymen being employed with clerics as trustees.

The church decided to implement rules and regulations to ensure that all of the Catholic Church's laws and principles were carried out.

The church's bishop was now required to approve the election and removal of all laymen and clerics as trustees. The new rules required that the bishop have authority over the details of their administration.

In the nearby country of Holland, laymen were still permitted to share in the responsibilities of the administration without direct supervision of the bishop.

The bishop was still to nominate the members but the priest was to preside over their position. Trustees were allowed to hold office for four years and were able to be reappointed at the end of their term.

When there was a vacancy two names were given to the bishop to be approved. He also had the authority to dismiss the whole board.

The practice of trustee-ism spread throughout the United States at a very early period. Rebellion quickly arose between the United States and the ecclesiastical authorities of the Catholic Church.

The central government headed by the pope, the Holy See, intervened to restore peace. New regulations and appointments were declared to restore the rights of the church against the dishonesty of the trustees.

The bishop of the church now had authority to decide their number and manner of appointment. The trustees selected for nomination should be men that have made their Easter duty, who contributed to the support of the church, and who sent their children to Catholic schools.

They were not permitted to work on the trustee board if they were members of prohibited societies. In the United States, differences varied when it came to the legal rights of trustees.

Members of the congregation had no authority to control the actions of the trustees contrary to the church regulations.

This includes the exercise of judgment of the officers as long as they did not violate bylaws. The legal rights of the bishop rested upon the ecclesiastical law. Serving as legal officers of the church, trustees have the power to hold title, mortgage, lease, sell, exchange, or rent church property.

Because church trustees handle the real property affairs of the church; it is a must that they are familiar with regulations of state and local municipal laws. State laws require that church organizations appoint board members to set bylaws and provisions concerning the terms of office, procedures for elections and their duties.

Each corporation, according to the Model Nonprofit Corporation Act, must elect a president, vice president, secretary, treasurer, and other officers. The other members of the board are allowed to hold more than one office.

According to state law, the church congregation has the authority to remove any member for a cause, whether it is stated or not stated in the church bylaws.

I will list a few causes that should cause a trustee to be disappointed (removed) from the ministry: doctrinal deviation, conduct unacceptable to church custom and practice, and incompetence and incapacity.

Incorporated churches must use the name of the organization on legal documents and never the names of the trustees. This is not a good practice because people have a tendency to leave church for little or no reason.

It is a United States Supreme Court ruling that a board of directors should manage all affairs of a corporation. In contrast the Church trustees only have the authority to perform duties as stated in the church's bylaws.

They have implied authority to do all that is necessary to carry out their ministry duties. At no point are the members of the trustee board to act as individuals when making executive decisions.

Many churches have failed to adopt this ruling and those that are unincorporated derive no authority from state law. Trustees and other board directors are never authorized to perform any duties not stated in the churches bylaws.

They are powerless to amend or make any changes of any church articles without the necessary consent of the pastor and local church body.

All members should be in attendance to handle business dealings. But if all cannot be present a decision can be made by what is known as a quorum.

A quorum is a number or percentage of the total authorized members that must be present in order for the board to transact business.

If this quorum is satisfied the business of the trustee ministry is valid as it would be for a general church meeting.

There are many different areas for which a trustee can offer his/her services. They are selected to do physical ministry primary, but in some setting that are ask to assist in making financial and investment decisions.

There are many types of TRUSTEES/TRUST COMPANIES: Trustees are used by secular corporate institutions, in foreclosure sales, bankruptcy settlements and signing legal documents.

A trust company manages assets for individuals and businesses. They owe the same fiduciary responsibilities to their client and must follow all guidelines stated in their trusts.

I. Chapter One

(What Is A Church Trustee?)

A Church Trustee supervises and maintains all real and personal property belonging to local church congregation so that the ministries of the congregation can be effective.

This includes any and all properties that directly support the public worship, general purposes and ministries of the church body.

A church trustee is also an investment manager of which involves the local church in possible financial investments. The Trustee as authorized by local church congregation can receive trusts, wills, and monetary gifts given to the congregation by its membership or other outside identity.

Trustees must remain subordinate to the church and pastor, as it relates to the job descriptions outlined in the church's bylaws. Trustees' are the gatekeepers and protector the church's property.

It is appropriate that Trustees assist in setting the church bylaws, procedures concerning corporate operations (state non-profit, tax exempt laws and local statues), building structures and loan applications.

The Trustee must possess sound judgment skills and special knowledge of investment principles and procedures. The trustees' are authorized to sign all legal documents concerning property and financial transactions after the approval of the local church body.

Trustees must also deliver contracts that facilitate the needs of any legal transaction (contracts). Trustees must submit honest reports to executive board, pastor and local congregation as it relates to all matters for which they have been duly assigned by the local congregation.

The Trustee holds a tremendous position of trust -- within the church. They must make sure that the monies, accounts, organization and related plans are carried out with the highest integrity and honesty.

The Trustee must be accountable for being honest in the operational process of the trustee ministry. They must know the Word of God. Some examples that show the office are Romans 16: 23, "Gaius mine host, and of the whole church, saluteth you. Erastus the chamberlain of the city saluteth you, and Quartus a brother." Probably one of the best examples is:

Ephesians 6:21-22-"*But that ye also may know my affairs, and how I do, Tychicus, a beloved brother and faithful minister in the Lord, shall make known to you all things; Whom I have sent unto you for the same purpose, that ye might know our affairs, and that he might comfort your hearts.*"

II. Chapter 2

(What Are The Necessary Traits Of Trustees?)

What are Traits? Traits are qualities, character, persona or behavior of a person. Therefore the…

Trustees must be **honest** (practical, discreet, wise, far-sighted or cautions), sometimes described as prudent individuals. Why? Because, they are holding a position that carries a responsibility that requires a thick skin.

Trustees adopt a legal liability for the property that they oversee and are held to a higher standard to be loyal, be of good faith, and trust.

Trustees must remember that they are never to place their own personal interest before the church request. Trustees must keep a prudent composure and carry themselves at a higher standard.

Trustees must be committed to the vision of the pastor and must at all times promote the church's vision. A trustee is a valuable asset for the church.

It is most important that the Trustee have an intimate relationship with the Lord Jesus Christ—that is, be born again and filled with the Holy Spirit.

No one should be allowed to serve in this position, just because they have plenty money, numerous assets, serve on an administrative level in the corporate world, or hold a political position—this servants must be spiritual!

Not only that, persons who serve in this ministry must financially support the local church as liberal givers. It is one thing to supervise over the assets of the church; yet it is another thing to serve and not be a participant—this must not be!

Not only that, persons who serve in this ministry must attend local church worship and teaching service. The trustee must attend bible study and seminars for advancing the tools of being a church trustee.

A Trustee must carry traits of a good leader and a team player. To encourage others, the trustee must possess the qualities they are trying to incorporate into their team. They must know how to delegate authoritatively and have an enthusiastic approach to their work.

They must stay confident, have self-control and be disciplined while displaying mutual respect for the ideas and opinions of others.

III. Chapter 3

(Can Anyone Become A Trustee?)

This may sound like a simple question, but over the years that I have pastured churches I have heard some say, "Anyone can be a trustee".

You may disagree, but I do not believe that anyone can be a church trustee. Even though this is not a biblical position as that of a pastor, bishop, elder, teacher or deacon; yet its functions are vital in today's advance complexities of business.

There are some exceptions to that rule. The trustee must be a person of character, integrity, sound spiritual morals and ethics.

Any acts of dishonesty or deception on the part of the trustee made while executing this ministry can be fatal to the advancement and life of the local church.

A dishonest or deceptive trustee cannot be tolerated. Before anyone is allowed to serve in this ministry, they need have some knowledge in building construction, building codes, building contractors, design drawing, and finance.

Being a trustee is a worthwhile commitment. A trustee should be chosen for what he or she can contribute to the organization and never for popularity.

To be an efficient trustee, he or she must be willing and able to give sufficient time and effort to the church as it relates primarily to the church property.

Again, relevant experience and skill should be taken into consideration. If someone is willing and have the correct mindset and attitude, these skills can be taught to them through lectures and seminars.

What I am implying is, do not disqualify someone just because they lack one or two of the above mentioned skills—if they are open for learning—train them!

IV. Chapter 4

(What Are The Church Trustees Duties?)

Church Trustees play an important role in the everyday functionality of their church's organization. The basic duties of a trustee involve the repairing, collection, management and investment of the local church's property.

Trustees must fulfill all tasks with special care to make sure all objectives are properly carried out and comply with church bylaws and policies.

Trustee are obligated to follow the instructions of the leadership and the congregation, while using extreme care and diligence when performing his or her duties.

Trustees should anticipate any disputes or conflicts and rectify them immediately. As you are aware, in business conflicts will arise. Yet when this does happen the trustee must not lose his/her temperament.

Trustees is responsible for assuring that the church building; also vans/buses, are properly functioning and ready to receive disciples and visitors.

It is the responsibility of the Trustee Ministry to report to the pastor and congregation with regard to all updates or repairs to the local plant.

The Trustee Ministry in some local churches are responsible for maintaining adequate insurance coverage and pay taxes on all properties and keeping all incorporations requirement up to date.

The Trustees Ministry is responsible for issuing annual budget requests for financial acquisitions, improvements, and property management.

The Local Church elects trustees to convey land for the usage of the congregation. This includes the purchase or construction of burial grounds, parsonages, schools, and the pastors living quarters…etc.

At no time should this ministry act independently of the wishes of the pastor and local congregation. That is to, sell property, add to the physical plant, purchase property, assume loans or tear down building(s) without the consent of the pastor and local church congregation.

The Trustee must be people of prayer. That is, always seeking the guidance of God, as it relates to executing one's duties.

The Trustee is legally and spiritually responsible for everything that goes on in and outside the church pertaining to proper functioning practices.

Epaphroditus was trusted (trustee) with the offering that had been raised for Paul, and it was his sole responsibility to make sure it got to Paul.

A Trustee must be completely surrendered to God in their life even though the ministry deals with secular situation a good sound biblical intellect is a must.

The Trustee Ministry must not be drive only by the intellect of men, but most by the intellect of the Scriptures.

In essence, a trustee is responsible for all the real and personal properties of the church. They have authority and a grave responsibility to properly follow the laws of the land and the laws of Scripture.

A fantastic trustee will make sure the laws of the land and the laws of Scripture are partners in the growth of the church, not adversaries. They have a responsibility over the funds of the church and must maintain ethical and sound business principles.

V. Chapter 5

(Examples of Church Trustee Duties)

As stated previously, a church trustee performs several functions in this ministry, but one is administrating.

An administrator's job is to organize, plan, and add structure to meet the churches overall objective. It is a good practice to always remaining open to the final wishes of the local congregation.

As a trustee must map the path from where the church is to where it needs to be as it relates to accomplishing the vision of the church.

This is done through strategic planning in relation to short and long-term goals. There is a saying, **"If you do not properly plan; you are planning to fail"**. The bible teaches us to count up the cost.

The trustee has an obligation to develop strategies to protect the interest of the congregation while minimizing financial risks.

If your church is incorporated with your secretary of state department, the Trustees or any one individual are not susceptible to legal claims filed against the church.

If your church is not in-corporate, you open up the trustee ministry, pastor, assistant pastor, executive board and others officer to lawsuits filed against the church.

I encourage you to **INCORPPRATE YOUR CHURCH.** Now, this is not the same as filing for a **501 (c) 3 Tax Exempt Status.** The two are different identities.

Incorporating your church is file with your state government. Tax Exempting your church is file with the Federal Government. I would also like to remind you that your Federal Tax Identification is file with the Federal Government.

I am not a church law or tax attorney, but if your church is sued it is the responsibility of the trustee ministry to handle all legal claims.

I am not saying that they are responsible for adjudicating the claim, but securing the proper qualified persons (attorney) to handle to the matter.

VI. Chapter 6

(Is the church trustee appointment position or calling of God?)

A church Trustee is an appointed position even though this person (male or female) should be a born again believer, practicing the biblical of giving tithing and offering to the local church.

A person is said to have a calling when they experience a strong and inner impulse toward a particular course of action due to a conviction of divine intervention.

God, the divine intervention, gives us gifts and talents that are to be used effectively for the church or for God's willed to be carried out.

These talents can range from the ability to speak to large groups of people, to motivate and drive people to act, or to be a lending hand to those in need. Each has its place in the church ministry.

You may disagree with this point of view, but in all of the research that I have exhausted; I have not found any information that affirms that God directly call people into the **"Trustee Ministry"**.

Many will enter into the Trustee Ministry but the resounding motivating drive should be that of loving God and the local church.

Once a person acknowledges that they are willing to accept the appointment into the **"Trustee Ministry"** there must be a comprehensive training period to ensure that all the aspects of understanding the "**Trustee Ministry**" has been exhausted. Trustees are appointed by the pastor, executive board or a member of the laxity.

Always remember that before these persons are **appointed** to serve as Trustees, the local congregation must be allowed to participate in the process.

Their opinions might be negative sometimes, but they are a part of the "**Church Family**". This will bring **less dissention** in the "Church Family", of which, allowing it to move forward in **peace and harmony**.

VII. Chapter 7

(Do's and Don'ts of the Church Trustee)

(Do's)

- Do mortgage lease rent or sell property
- Can invest funds for clients while minimizing financial risks
- Do act in good faith, be honest, and loyal
- Place beneficiaries interest before those of their own.
- Do establish bookkeeping procedures
- Must comply applicable church bylaws and policies
- Do Avoid conflicts of interest
- Do act on fiduciary duties to the client
- Do take responsibility for legal actions and claims
- Do keep adequate records of all transactions

(Don'ts)

- Do not comingle client restricted funds.

- Do not lease church property without consent of congregation.
- Do not break or breach any contracts or organization bylaws.
- Do not accept gifts or hospitality without church consent.
- Never make loans without proper documentation and security clearances.
- Do not perform acts not authorized by either state law.

- Do not make any decisions as an individual.
- Never take title in personal name without designating yourself as trustee.
- Do not try gain or benefit directly or indirectly from a trust of the Local church.

VIII. Conclusion

The Ministry of The Church Trustee is a very demanding responsibility and it requires honesty, integrity, character, commitment and diligent.

I would like to encourage all who serve in this ministry to serve well and always have the mindset of that of servant (waiter).

There are too many people who look at this ministry for the perspective of **POWER**, rather than one of bring a **SERVANT**. God has blessed you and graced you with a talent or gift—used it to glorify him and bless his church.

Trustees you must handle all business transactions in good faith, confidence, loyalty, and honesty while expressing due diligence, unanimity, and show duty of care.

In closing, serve well and the Lord will reward you with the words of **"Well Done Thy Good And Faithful Servant"**.

God Bless,

Joseph R. Rogers, Sr., D. Min.

IX. Trustee Code of Conduct

As a Trustee of the _____ Church, I promise to abide by standards of Scriptures, the Churches Constitution/Bylaws and Laws of this (federal, state and local) while serving and executing my duties as a Trustee.

These are:

A. Accountability:

Everything _____ Church does is empowered to stand the test of scrutiny of challenges, criticism from all outside forces, and I will pledge to be accountable to God and this local church body in the same manner.

B. Integrity and Honesty:

These codes of conduct with the bible as foundation will be the hallmarks of all conduct when dealing with fellow disciples and with individuals and institutions outside this institution.

C. Openness:
_____ Church strives to maintain an atmosphere of openness throughout the organization to promote the image, character and integrity of the Trinity (Godhead) and I remain transparent in all of my dealings with this local church.

As a trustee, I also pledge to maintain truthfulness in:

1. Law, mission, policies of this church:

**I will not break the law or breach charity regulations in any aspect of my role as a trustee.

**I will support the mission and consider myself its guardian.

**I will abide by all organizational policies and status of this state; as I also follow the Holy Scriptures.

2. Conflicts of interest:

**I will always strive to act in the best interests of the organization.

**I will declare any conflict of interest, or any circumstances that might be viewed by others as a conflict of interest, as soon as it arises.

**I will submit to the judgment of God, this

church and fellow board members and do as it is required regarding potential conflicts of interest.

3. Person to person:

**I will not break the law, breach charity regulations or act in disregard of organizational policies in my relationships with fellow trustees, Christian or church disciple, staff, volunteers, members, service recipients, contractors or anyone I come into contact with in my role as a trustee.

**I will strive to establish respectful, collegial and courteous relationships with all I come into contact with in my role as trustee.

4. Protecting the organization's reputation:

**I will not speak as a trustee of this organization to the media or in a public forum without the prior knowledge and approval of the Chair or Chief Executive.

**When I am speaking as a trustee of this organization, my comments will reflect current organizational policy even when these do not agree with my personal views.

**When speaking as a private citizen I will strive to uphold the reputation of the Lord Jesus and the local church integrity, remembering that even in this capacity, my responsibility to the organization is not diminished. I will respect organizational, Board and fellow disciple's confidentiality.

5. Personal gain:

**I will not personally gain materially or financially from my role as a trustee, nor will I permit others to do so as a result of my actions or negligence.

**I will document expenses and seek reimbursement according to procedure.

**I will not accept substantial gifts or hospitality

without prior consent of the Chair.

**I will use organizational resources responsibly, when authorized, in accordance with procedure.

5. In the boardroom

**I will strive to embody the principles of leadership in all my actions and live up to the trust placed within me as an appointed trustee.

**I will abide by Trustee Board governance procedures and practices.

**I will strive to attend all Trustee Board meetings, giving the Chair and/or other board member enough notice if I am unable to attend.

**I will study the agenda and other information sent to me in good time prior to the meeting and be prepared to debate and vote on agenda items during the meeting.

**I will honor the authority of the Chair and respect his or her role as meeting leader.

**I will engage in debate and voting in meetings according to procedure, maintaining a respectful attitude toward the opinions of others while making my voice heard.

**I will accept a majority Trustee Board vote on an issue as decisive and final.

**I will maintain confidentiality about what goes on in the boardroom unless authorized by the Chair or Trustee Board Members to speak of it.

6. Enhancing governance

**I will participate in training and development activities for trustees.

**I will continually seek ways to improve Trustee Board governance practice.

**I will strive to identify good candidates for

trusteeship and appoint new trustees on the basis of merit.

**I will support the Chair in his/her efforts to improve his/her leadership skills.

**I will support the Chief Executive in his/her executive role and, with my fellow Board members, seek development opportunities for him/her.

7. Leaving the board

**I understand that substantial breach of any part of this code may result in my removal from the trustee board.

**Should I resign from the Board I will inform the Chair in advance in writing, stating my reasons for resigning. Additionally, I will participate in an exit interview.

Signed:_____

Name:_____

Date:_____

X. The Work Book Section

(Introduction)

1. Though the "_____ _____" is necessary for the effective and efficient operation of a local church body, it is not a _____ _____.

2. The Trustees are a _____ mandate whose responsibility is to the physical property of the church.

3. The role of a church trustee is described as being a _____ _____ over God's household affairs.

4. The Church Trustee's are managers of God's property at the leading of the church congregation.

    True_____   False_____

5. The Trustees main responsibility is to model and teach principles of _____ _____.

6. The trustee demonstrates _____ _____ skills and judgment as it relates to the church's property.

7. The Trustees function as the _____ of the church and as a communication link between _____, executive board, board of directors and _____ of the congregation.

8. The trustee system dates back to the _____ in the Catholic Church in the _____ _____.

9. Its purpose and duties are somewhat _____ today. At its conception the _____ _____l of Carthage requested that the civil power appoint five officers for their current _____ _____.

10. The employment of trustees or laymen with clerics became the _____ all over the country.

11. In England they were called _____- _____ and were chosen by the parish priest and parishioners.

12. The Trustees administered the temporalities of the parish under the direct supervision of the churches' bishop.

    True_____   False_____

13. As trustee-ism spread throughout the nation the church began to have _____ with laymen being employed with _____ as trustees.

14. The church decided to implement _____ and _____ to ensure that all of the Catholic Church's laws and principles were carried out.

15. The church's bishop was now required to _____ the election and removal of all _____ and _____ as trustees.

16. The new rules required that the bishop have authority over the details of their administration.

True_____   False_____

17. In the nearby country of _____, laymen were still permitted to share in the responsibilities of the administration without _____ supervision of the bishop.

18. The bishop was still to _____ the members but the priest was to preside over their position.

19. Trustees were allowed to hold office for four years and were able to be reappointed at the end of their term.

True_____   False_____

20. The practice of _____-ism spread throughout the United States at a very _____ period.

21. Rebellion quickly arose between the United States and the _____ authorities of the Catholic Church.

22. The central government headed by the_____, the Holy See, intervened to restore peace.

23. The bishop of the church now had _____ to decide their number and manner of appointment.

24. In the United States, _____ varied when it came to the legal rights of trustees.

25. Members of the _____ had no authority to control the actions of the trustees contrary to the church _____.

26. Because church trustees handle the real _____ affairs of the church; it is a must that they are familiar with _____ of state and local municipal laws.

27. State laws require that church organizations appoint _____ _____ to set bylaws and provisions concerning the terms of office, procedures for elections and their duties.

28. Each corporation, according to the Model Nonprofit Corporation Act, must elect a _____, vice president, _____, treasurer, and other officers.

29. The other members of the board are allowed to hold _____ than one office.

30. According to state law, the church congregation has the authority to remove any member for a cause, whether it is stated or not stated in the church bylaws.

   True_____   False_____

31. Incorporated churches must use the name of the organization on legal _____ and never the names of the _____.

32. This is not a good practice because people have a tendency to leave church for little or no reason.

   True_____   False_____

33. It is a United States Supreme Court _____ that a board of directors should _____ all affairs of a corporation.

34. In contrast the Church trustees only have the authority to _____ duties as stated in the church's _____.

35. At no point are the members of the trustee board to act as _____ when making executive decisions.

36. Many churches have _____ to adopt this ruling and those that are unincorporated derive _____ authority from state law.

37. Trustees and other board directors are never _____ to perform any duties not stated in the _____ bylaws.

38. They are _____ to amend or make any changes of any church articles without the necessary _____ of the pastor and local church body.

39. All members should be in attendance to handle business dealings.

    True_____   False_____

40. But if all cannot be present a decision can be made by what is known as a _____.

41. A _____ is a number or percentage of the total authorized members that must be present in order for the board to transact business.

42. If this quorum is _____ the business of the trustee ministry is valid as it would be for a general church meeting.

43. The Trustees are selected to do _____ _____ primary, but in some setting that are ask to assist in making _____ and _____ decisions.

44. There are many types of _____/_____ _____: Trustees are used by secular corporate institutions, in foreclosure sales, bankruptcy settlements and signing legal documents.

45. A trust company manages assets for individuals and businesses.

   True_____   False_____

46. Trustees owe the same _____ responsibilities to their client and must follow all guidelines stated in their trusts.

Chapter One

(What Is A Church Trustee?)

1. A church trustee _____ and _____ all real and personal property belonging to local church congregation so that the ministries of the congregation can be effective.

2. This includes any and all _____ that directly support the public worship, general purposes and ministries of the church body.

3. A church trustee is also an _____ manager of which involves the local church in possible financial investments.

4. The Trustee as _____ by local church congregation can receive trusts, wills, and monetary gifts given to the congregation by its membership or other outside identity.

5. Trustees must remain _____ to the church and pastor, as it relates to the job descriptions outlined in the church's bylaws.

6. Trustees' are the gatekeepers and protector the church's property.

    True_____   False_____

7. The Trustee must possess sound _____ skills and special knowledge of investment principles and _____.

8. The trustees' are _____ to sign all legal documents concerning _____ and _____ transactions after the approval of the local church body.

9. Trustees must submit _____ reports to executive board, pastor and local congregation as it relates to _____ matters for which they have been duly _____ by the local congregation.

10. The Trustee holds a tremendous position of trust – within the church.

    True_____   False_____

11. The Trustees must make sure that the monies, accounts, organization and related plans are carried out with the highest _____ and _____.

12. The Trustee must be _____ for being honest in the operational process of the trustee ministry.

13. They must know the Word of God. Some examples that show the office are _____ 16: 23, "Gaius mine host, and of the whole church, saluteth you. Erastus the chamberlain of the city saluteth you, and Quartus a brother."

Chapter Two, Three & Four

(Chapter 2)

(What Are The Necessary Traits Of Trustees?)

1. What are Traits? Traits are _____,
_____, persona or behavior of a person.

2. Trustee must be _____ (practical,
discreet, wise, far-sighted or cautions), sometimes
described as prudent individuals..

3. The Trustees are to adopt a _____ liability
for the property that they oversee and are held to a
_____ standard to be loyal, be of good faith,
and trust.

4. The Trustees must remember that they are never to
place their own _____ interest before the
church request.

5. Trustees must keep a _____ composure and
carry themselves at a higher standard.

6. The Trustees must be committed to the _____ of
the pastor and must at all times promote the church's
_____.

7. A trustee is a valuable asset for the church.

   True_____   False_____

8. It is most important that the Trustee have an _____ relationship with the Lord Jesus Christ—that is, be born again and filled with the Holy Spirit.

9. No Trustee should be allowed to serve in this position, just because they have plenty _____, numerous _____, serve on an administrative level in the corporate world, or hold a _____ position—this servants must be spiritual!

10. The Trustee who serves in this ministry must _____ support the local church as _____ givers.

11. It is one thing to _____ over the assets of the church; yet it is another thing to _____ and not be a participant—this must not be!

12. The Trustees must attend local church _____ and _____ service.

13. The Trustees attend _____ _____ and _____ for advancing the tools of being a church trustee.

14. A trustee must carry traits of a good leader and a _____ player.

15. A Trustee must stay _____, have self-control and be _____ while displaying mutual respect for the ideas and opinions of others.

Chapter 3

(Can Anyone Become A Trustee?)

1. It has been said over the years that I have pastured churches I have heard some say, **"Anyone can be a trustee".**

True_____   False_____

2. The Trustee is not a_____ position as that of a pastor, bishop, elder, teacher or deacon; yet its functions are vital in today's advance complexities of business.

3. The trustee must be a person of _____, _____, sound spiritual morals and ethics.

4. A dishonest or _____ trustee cannot be tolerated.

5. Being a trustee is a _____ _____ commitment.

6. A trustee should be chosen for what he or she can contribute to the organization and never for

_____.

7. To be an efficient trustee, he or she must be _____ and able to give _____ time and effort to the church as it relates primarily to the church property.

8. _____ experience and skill should be taken into consideration.

Chapter 4

(What Are The Church Trustees Duties?)

1. Church trustees play an important role in the everyday _____ of their church's organization.

2. The _____ duties of a trustee involve the repairing, collection, management and investment of the local church's property.

3. A trustee is _____ to follow the instructions of the leadership and the congregation, while using extreme care and diligence when performing his or her duties.

4. Trustees should _____ any disputes or conflicts and rectify them immediately. As you are aware, in business _____ will arise.

5. The trustee must not lose his/her temperament.

    True_____   False_____

6. The trustee is responsible for _____ that the church building; also vans/buses, are properly functioning and ready to receive disciples and visitors.

7. It is the responsibility of the Trustee Ministry to _____ to the pastor and congregation with regard to all _____ or _____ to the local plant.

8. Trustee Ministry in some local churches are responsible for maintaining _____ insurance coverage and pay taxes on all _____ and keeping all incorporations requirement up to date.

9. Trustees Ministry is responsible for _____ annual budget requests for financial acquisitions, improvements, and property management.

10. The Local Church elects trustees to _____ land for the usage of the congregation.

11. The Trustee must never sell property, add to the physical plant, purchase property, assume loans or tear down building(s) without the consent of the pastor and local church congregation.

   True_____   False_____

12. The Trustee must be people of _____. That is, always seeking the _____ of God, as it relates to executing one's duties.

13. The Trustee is _____ and _____ responsible for everything that goes on in and outside the church _____ to proper functioning practices.

14. _____ was trusted (trustee) with the offering that had been raised for Paul, and it was his sole responsibility to make sure it got to Paul.

15. Trustees must be _____ surrendered to God in their life even though the ministry deals with secular situation a good sound biblical intellect is a must.

16. The Trustee Ministry must not be drive only by the _____ of men, but most by the intellect of the _____.

17. In essence, a trustee is _____ for all the real and personal properties of the church.

18. The Trustees has _____ and a grave _____ to properly follow the laws of the land and the laws of Scripture.

19. A Trustee will make sure the _____ of the land and the laws of _____ are partners in the growth of the church, not adversaries.

20. The Trustees have a responsibility over the _____ of the church and must maintain _____ and _____ business principles.

Chapter Five

(Examples of Church Trustee Duties)

1. The Trustee as an administrator is to
_____, _____, and add
structure to meet the churches overall
_____.

2. As a trustee must _____ the _____
from where the church is to where it needs to be as it
relates to accomplishing the vision of the church.

 3. This is done through _____ planning in
relation to _____ and long-term goals.

4. There is a saying, "If you do not _____
plan; you are _____ to fail".

5. The trustee has an _____ to develop
strategies to protect the _____ of the
congregation while minimizing financial risks.

5. If your church is _____ with your
secretary of state department, the Trustees or any one
individual are not _____ to legal claims
filed against the church.

6. If your church is not _____,
you open up the trustee ministry, pastor, assistant
pastor, executive board and others officer to
_____ filed against the church.

7. This author encourages churches to **INCORPPRATE YOUR CHURCH.**

True_____   False_____

 8. INCORPPRATE YOUR CHURCH and 501 © 3 Tax Exempt Status are the same identities.

True_____   False_____

9. Incorporating your church is file with your state
_____.

10. Tax Exempting your church is file with the
_____ Government.

Chapter 6

(Is the church trustee appointment position or calling of God?)

1. A church trustee is an _____ position even though this person (male or female) should be a born again _____, practicing the biblical method of giving _____ and _____ to the local church.

2. God, the _____ intervention, gives us gifts and talents that are to be used _____ for the church or for God's willed to be carried out.

3. These talents can range from the _____ to speak to large groups of people, to _____ and drive people to act, or to be a _____ hand to those in need. Each has its place in the church ministry.

4. Trustees are _____ by the pastor, executive board or a member of the laxity.

5. The Trustee Ministry participates must be _____ in their motivating drive should be that of _____ God and the local church.

6. There must be a _____ training period for those who are to become trustees to ensure that all the aspects of _____ the "Trustee Ministry" are exhausted.

Chapter 7

(Do's and Don'ts of the Church Trustee & Conclusion)

(Do's & Don'ts)

A. List Five (5) of The Do's of The Trustee Ministry

1._____
_____
_____

2._____
_____
_____

3._____
_____
_____

4._____
_____
_____

5._____
_____
_____

B. List Five (5) of The Don't's of The Trustee Ministry

1._____
_____
_____

2. _____

_____

_____

3. _____

_____

_____

4. _____

_____

_____

5. _____

_____

_____

(Conclusion)

1. The Ministry of The Church Trustee is a very _____ responsibility and it requires honesty, integrity, character, commitment and diligent.

2. There are too many people who look at this ministry for the perspective of _____, rather than one of bring a _____.

3. God has blessed you and graced you with a talent or gift—used it to _____ him and _____ his church.

4. Trustee's you must handle all business transactions with _____ _____, confidence, loyalty, and _____ while expressing due diligence, unanimity, and show duty of care.

5. Serve well and the Lord will _____ you with the words of **"Well Done Thy Good And Faithful Servant"**.

XI. Author's Contact Information & Other Works

Mailing Address:

1313 Ujamaa Drive, Raleigh, NC 27610

Phone Nos. (919) 208-0200

Email Address:

jroger3420@aol.com

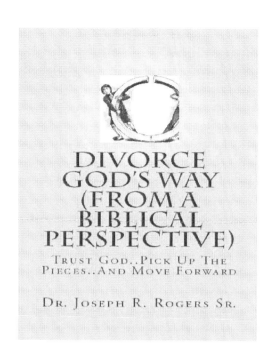

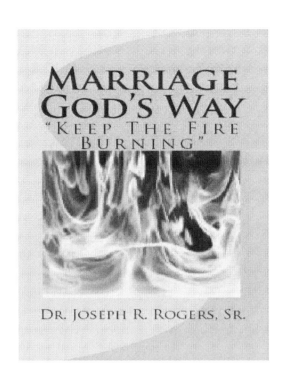

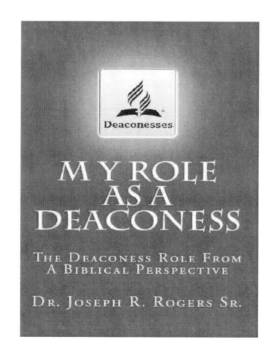

(There Is A Series of 1-39)

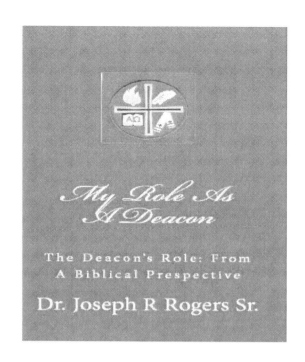

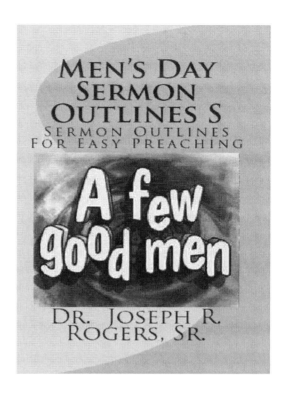

Mother's/Women's Day Sermon Series S

Happy MOTHER'S DAY

Dr. Joseph Roosevelt Rogers, Sr.

MINISTERING TO THE SENIORS Dr. Joseph R. Rogers Sr.

"THE DAYS OF OUR YEARS ARE THREESCORE YEARS AND TEN; AND IF BY REASON OF STRENGTH THEY BE FOURSCORE YEARS". (PSALMS 90:10A)

Graceful Seniors

MINISTERING TO THE SENIORS

Understanding The Myths & Truths Of The Aging Process

DR. JOSEPH R. ROGERS SR.

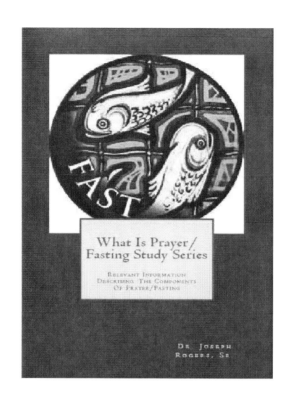

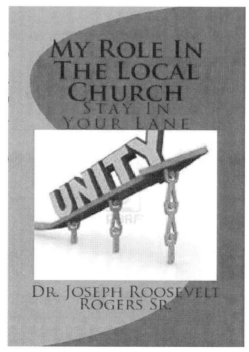

XII. Notes